I0484842

# 2015
# Business Plan


## Submitted
## January 31, 2015


by
**Thomas Mindala**
**(President / CEO TRAIN2WIN LLC)**

# Table of Contents

# Mission Statement

Our mission is to use the skills and techniques we have to help others design the training tools they need, while never forgetting that it is our clients who know best what their team members need to learn and know.

Our philosophy is that the client always comes first in all that we do, and it is the client who will decide what it is that we will do.

# Goals & Objectives

Here's what we've managed to accomplish during our first 9 months in business:

- We established the basic framework and a dynamic image for the business.

- We validated that image through the recommendations of associates.

- We set up and established the financial side of the company based on the legal requirements of a Limited Liability Company (LLC) with the necessary forms for management and reporting purposes.

- We set up a working webpage for the company that aligns itself well with the image we created (Train2win.weebly.com).

- We developed a model for how we plan to distribute the ideas and services we offer through the books and publications tools on Amazon.com.

- We've made much progress in the development of published materials.

- We made effective use of social media (Linked In) to promote the business.

- Successfully worked within the targeted $1000.00 start-up investment.

Our goals and objectives for 2015 will remain cautious for the most part with an eye towards staying within a well defined and limited budget that allows us to continue to build the published infrastructure of the business which will create a solid foundation for the future as we look for potential clients for our programs and services.

- The 2015 budget will stress the creation and continued development of the tools needed (publications on Amazon.com, marketing packet, etc.) to promote the business while we continue to search for clients willing to pay.

  The ideal objective by the end of 2015 is to reach a breakeven point between our start-up costs and ongoing expenses, and the revenue coming into the budget through purchased publications and a paying client.

- Complete the basic infrastructure of published materials for the identified key training tools and programs we plan to offer potential clients.

- Offer focused and cost effective services that include both the combined programs and ala cart tools we created in 2014, the specific services communicated in the TRAIN2WIN Publications Series, and what should become available in the Coach2win and Speak2win programs still in development.

- Use our available processes through social media and networked associations to identify and promote our unique services to prospective clients.

- The ultimate goal for 2015 will be to find that one client willing to pay for our services and work with us to field test and validate our ideas and what we know to be true.

During 2014 we've experienced some "fits and starts" of progress as awareness of and interest in TRAIN2WIN continues to spread. We've actually sold a few books on Amazon.com. Most of the interest in truth has related to somebody wishing to sell me some item or service, but there has also been honest interest in partnering here and there in various ways, and there has even been a couple of job offers for me to come to work.

Everything we do during 2015, especially where it relates to the revenue and expense budget, must reflect and stay closely aligned to the goals and objectives stated here and throughout this business plan.

Changes to our objectives and goals for 2015 must be approved by both members of the board (myself and Jennifer) and be supported by the potential opportunities that they represent.

We will stay dedicated to our goals and objectives while we at the same time remain flexible enough to see and take advantage of opportunities as they present themselves.

# Updated Market Analysis

- Current situation
- Opportunities
- Niche
- Focus 2015

### (1)  Current Situation

2015 appears to be a time when the economy as a whole is entering a more confident stage that will support both continued growth as well as a better business climate for an increased investment on infrastructure by companies and organizations in general.  Not only is the stock market performing well, but consumer confidence is rising as a result of lower than expected energy costs.

Many companies have been holding onto cash reserves out of a reluctance to overly invest in an unstable business climate.  With growing confidence as a result of improving budget and profit performances during 2014 company executive management teams are now more willing to spend than they have been since the spring of 2009 when the US economy went into a near collapse.

### (2)  Opportunities

The increased confidence and willingness to spend cash reserves on upgrading corporate infrastructures by executive management teams includes a high priority in many cases on improving the training offered to employees.  While the largest companies have the capabilities within their own corporate structure to provide the improved training they desire, many small to large companies lack the in house ability to do so.  In most of these cases the executive management team typically looks outside the organization to find a "consultant partner" to help them deliver the training they are looking for.

### (3)  Niche

In continuation of the original TRAIN2WIN Business Plan as created in January of 2014, the 2015 Plan places a strong emphasis on providing a set of services designed to fit a specific "niche" within the corporate training industry.

- Work with small to medium size corporate clients to design customized and cost effective employee training tools in specific areas.

- Continue to rely on the "Train the Trainer" model for the foreseeable future where we help create and design the training program tool, then teach and coach those in the client organization to implement and manage the training themselves.

## (4) Focus 2015

Continue the focus in 2015 on key areas of organizational and employee based training initiatives that include the following:

- On-board training for new employees

- Sales and customer service training for field employees

- Change management and communications training for corporate executive management teams

- Harassment training tools and services

In addition to these identified areas of employee based training, we will also offer training opportunities for the following:

- Why training so often fails to provide the improvements we seek

- Instructional training to those making presentations to employees

- Instructional training for mentoring coaches

To do so, we will continue to focus on the creation of training materials (they are called TRAIN2WIN Publications) developed and made available for purchase on Amazon.com; and we will focus also on the development of companion Power Point Presentations for both sale and delivery where applicable and as the opportunities present themselves.

# Competitive Analysis

- **Consultant landscape**
- **Training consultants**
- **The ugly truth**
- **How we differ at TRAIN2WIN**
- **The opportunity**

## (1)  Consultant Landscape

The consulting business is a large and crowded industry that takes little more than a business card and fancy pitch to get on board and play.  This is more true in 2015 than ever due to 3 specific circumstances:

- Baby boomers have moved on from longstanding careers in droves to enter the field as consultants in a wide variety of industries.

- The rise of highly accessible computer based programs and systems have made it easier to launch and implement a credible business strategy with an impressive and professional looking portfolio.

- The weak economy over the past 5 years has driven a large number of highly skilled corporate managers into the consultant industry.

## (2)  Training Consultants

Like the consultant landscape in general, the field of training consultants is full of a wide variety of so called experts that include those with a national reputation as well as many well known local and regional players.  Typically consultants in the employee based training field offer the following:

- A glitzy well designed portfolio that offers specific training tools such as sales training, customer service training, operational training, harassment training, or change management training.

- What the typical training consultant does not offer is any sort of iron clad guarantee that what they do is a good fit for the client or that there will be measurable improvements that result from their efforts.

### (3)  The Ugly Truth

Based both on my own experiences and those of many other business professionals I've talked to over the years, there's an ugly truth about the vast majority of consultants which include the following observations:

- Consultants typically arrive on the scene when things are not going well and the executive management team is in search of "quick fix" solutions to the problems they identify.

- The typical consultant has a glitzy and impressive looking portfolio that demonstrates his or her credibility and the magic solutions his or her program promises to offer.

- In a shocking majority of cases, however, not only does the program offered and agreed to not work as promised, but the consultant has also managed to wiggle him or herself into the client organization in a manner that opens up additional "revenue stream opportunities."

- At the end of the day the client is left with a hefty bill to pay (usually higher than expected) with little or no real or measurable benefit.

- In many cases the training initiative mandated by the consultant has not only not resulted in the improvements desired, but has actually created additional morale issues and instability in the labor force.

- Executive management's left afterwards wondering what they paid for.

### (4)  How We Differ at TRAIN2WIN

We again refer to the moniker as stated in the original business plan last year that said **"TRAIN2WIN is a different kind of training partner"**

Once again this year, we will focus on the differentiation between the classic consultant and what we do at TRAIN2WIN in partnership with our clients.

- We are experts in the field of employee based training initiatives.

- We do have some preconceived ideas and philosophies regarding what training should look like and how it should be conducted.

- We do not, however, present the client with a prepackaged program based on preconceived ideas and assumptions that might or might not be a good fit or relevant to current realities.

- What we will do is sit down with clients to use our own experiences and expertise to help them create unique training tools designed for the specific needs and circumstances of their organization.

- All of what we do and have designed will be customized fully to what the customer needs and wants.

- All of the training tools we design will be as cost effective as possible to fit into the tight budget of small to medium size organizations and companies.

- All that we do and create will become the property of the client to use as they see fit in the future. All we ask is permission to use what we've helped create as examples for future clients.

## (5)  The Opportunity

The differentiation between the typical classic training consultant who arrives with a glitzy and expensive prepackaged and many times dysfunctional program as compared to the highly customizable and cost effective tools that we offer at TRAIN2WIN provides the opportunity to fill an existing niche in the training world that is currently expanding along with an improving business economy that's emerging from years of poor performance, instability, and low morale.

# Competitive Strategies

- Basic infrastructure
- Competitive focus
- Build the network
- Target a niche in the market
- Focus on customization and guarantees
- Targeted strategies
- Tactical considerations

## (1) Basic Infrastructure

The first priority during the first quarter of 2015 is to complete the basic infrastructure of the published services offered by the company. These include the identified training programs we are focusing on along with the respective publications and power point programs that are applicable. These include:

- TRAIN2WIN Manifesto: A statement of intent and philosophy (DONE)

- TRAIN2WIN Presentation Guide: What we offer and how we differ (DONE)

- TRAIN2WIN Publications Series: Short easy to read detailed discussions about specific employee based training issues (IN PROGRESS)

- TRAIN2WIN Welcome Aboard Training Program for the newly hired employee (IN PROGRESS)

- TRAIN2WIN Winning Customer Service Training Program for customer service field personnel (IN PROGRESS)

- TRAIN2WIN Sales to Win Training Program for sales personnel (IN PROGRESS)

- TRAIN2WIN Dynamic Change to Win Training Program for executive management teams (IN PROGRESS)

- TRAIN2WIN Coach to Win Training Program for organizations who wish to coach up employees with the specific skills they need (DONE)

Both the Manifesto and Presentation Guide need updated for 2015 and all other identified tools and materials need to be completed and published for use with potential clients by the end of the first quarter.

## (2) Competitive Focus

Our focus will continue to be on our expertise based on my many years of experience both in the field of operations and as a recognized training design and implementation manager at the national level.

We will continue to stress our uniqueness in the consultant world as a "different kind of consultant" by emphasizing our willingness to fully customize what we do to the customer's needs and expectations, our cost effectiveness, and our guaranteed services and programs.

## (3) Build the Network

Through our current business contacts, new contacts made, efforts through social media (Linked In, Facebook, and Google), word of mouth, published postings on Amazon.com, and a limited marketing campaign during 2015 we will continue to build a network of associations and potential clients.

## (4) Target a Niche in the Market

Our target customer is the small to medium size organization who lacks an in house capability (department) to design and implement employee based training initiatives on their own who are looking for cost effective and relevant alternatives and solutions. Our goal in 2015 is to identify and begin to reach out to prospective clients no later than the second or third quarter of the year.

## (5) Focus on Customization and Guarantees

We will keep and maintain our focus on our willingness and ability to fully customize what we do on a cost effective basis in a manner that stays closely aligned with what the client expects and needs.

We will continue to offer no nonsense guarantees with the "Opt Out" and "Guaranteed Performance" clauses we offer to clients in our service programs.

## (6) Targeted Strategies

- Continue to develop and use the Amazon.com based publications as a building revenue stream platform and focus of our marketing of ideas.
- Continue to use Linked In as a marketing tool to post and distribute information and hold discussions about things we identify as important.
- Revisit the Weekly.com website and determine what needs to be done to turn it into a relevant and effective tool to build the business.

- Use the Speak2win speakers bureau initiative concept as a potential marketing tool to get the word out by reaching out for opportunities to get myself in front of groups.

## (7) Tactical Considerations

- Possibly join community and / or business groups that can help promote the business (budget considerations here)

- Do "pro bono" work for identified organizations to use as a resume builder. Non-profit organizations might represent good potential opportunities.

- Do related volunteer work where the opportunity arises that can also help build the resume.

2015 will continue to be a transitional year as we begin to move the company from it's initial start-up position to a more stable position with the necessary platform essentials (infrastructure) in place to begin to reach out and grow the potential opportunities with credible client customers who should appear in an improving market place.

# Business Strategy

- **2014 results**
- **2015 expectations**
- **Revenue streams**
- **Expense profile**
- **Reporting**
- **Regulations**

### (1) 2014 Results

While 2014 proved to be a year where we did in fact successfully establish the company, build the beginnings of a functional operational framework and a dynamic image, put in place a firm business structure based on a "best practices" accounting approach, and made much progress in developing the published infrastructure we've worked hard to identify, it was also a year where we spent a total of $988.78 with revenues of only $36.74, which represents a loss of $952.04. All of which is due to start up costs and a planned cautious approach to marketing the business in its early stages, and was not unexpected.

### (2) 2015 Expectations

2015 needs to be a year where we at least make a huge dent if not completely close the gap of profitability for the business. We will continue to keep a tight control on expenses while we increase our efforts in search of credible paying clients and a functional revenue stream. Both will be done through our efforts to continue the development of published materials and programs, and the marketing of the business through social media and industry associations.

### (2) Revenue Streams

Our next priority for 2015 once our basic infrastructure is fully in place will be to establish a true revenue stream that actually helps develop a positive cash flow for the business and close the budget gap. Our primary focus will be as follows:

- Continue to develop published materials on Amazon.com and use social media to market their existence more aggressively.

- Research other possibilities that will allow the published materials to get more exposure. This will include a review of how to create a functional website that includes a direct link which allows those who visit it to purchase our publications (revisit the Weebly.com already in place site to try and improve its functionality).

- Continue to seek out additional more diversified revenue streams, specifically the search for that one paying client who buys one or more of our programs or tools. At the same time keep an eye on other potential revenue generating possibilities such as the proposed Speak2win speaker's bureau and Coach2win concepts.

**(3) Expense Profile**

- We will continue to maintain a tight control over expenses, and Jennifer will have the right of final approval for any major expenses.

- The primary expense categories for 2015 will include the continuation of proof copies for the publications being developed (estimated at $50.00 to $75.00 for the year), a usable marketing tool (About Us) to be distributed to targeted potential clients (estimated at $100.00 to $150.00), and some additional equipment to get the computer power point system up for use (estimated at not more than $150.00).

**(4) Reporting**

- We will continue to use the Expense & Revenue General Ledger as our primary expense to income tracking device in 2015.

- As "program buying" customer clients come onto line we will implement the Individual Client Ledger, Billing Invoice, and Income Statement tools to help us manage the financial side of the business.

- An annual report of Income to Expenses for 2015 will be completed and published no later than January 31, 2016.

**(5) Regulations**

- As revenue begins to be generated as projected during 2015 it will become essential to review and keep a close eye on all of the relevant reporting and tax regulations so that we establish and maintain the financial legalities of the business. This will be Jennifer's primary responsibility.

- We (Jennifer) will also need to research carefully all of the applicable IRS rules and regulations regarding how employee board members are compensated (i.e. Thomas and Jennifer).

# Management Strategy

- **Limited Liability Corporation (LLC)**
- **Leverage talents & network of associates**
- **Competitive pricing structure**

### (1)  Limited Liability Corporation (LLC)

For legal and tax purposes TRAIN2WIN LLC is and will continue to be a Limited Liability Corporation with a membership board that includes Thomas Mindala (President and CEO) and Jennifer Mindala (Chief Financial Officer).  There are no plans at this time to bring anybody else into the business structure, and / or add additional members to the board of directors.  As it stands, both Jennifer and myself are unpaid employees and board members.  There are no other paid employees and we need to research the IRS rules and regulations for this during the coming year (see #5 Regulations in the Business Strategy chapter).

While Jennifer will have the final say on all major expenditures, it will continue to be Thomas who runs and manages the business day to day and make the operational decisions where necessary.

During 2015 no less than 2 formal meetings of the membership board will be scheduled to discuss both the current status of the business along with any newly proposed strategies for the direction we need to go in the future.  The dates for these meetings will be communicated as necessary between the members of the board.

### (2)  Leverage Talents & Network of Associates

During 2015 we will continue to leverage my extensive experience, talents, and associations to build the credibility of the business.  During 2014 a loose network of business associations and partnerships were successfully established with a variety of selected industry business professionals and others who have and continue to be willing to offer their expertise, input, and suggestions as requested.  To date these associated partnerships are as follows:

- Jeff Child - Managing Director of National Paint Alliance

- Monte Dunbar - Computer network programming expert

- David H. Fruhling - Former CFO / COO of Fico Buzz Feed Inc.

- Jim Gamberg - Former Operations and Marketing Manager Comex USA

- Angela Hernquist - Director of Training CSU Online Digital University

- Cara Johnson - Vice President of Human Resources Comex USA

- Clayton Nattier - Mentor and self taught income tax expert

In addition to my work in developing the basic infrastructure (publications and programs) for the business, my primary role in 2015 will be to search for that one or two credible paying clients that will allow us to both test and refine our methods and ideas, and begin to build the revenue streams we need to be successful in the long term.

### (3) Competitive Pricing Structure

It will continue to be our goal in 2015 to not only establish but further refine a fair and competitive pricing and fee structure for all of our programs and services that meet the needs of the small and medium size organization at the same time they meet the needs of and support our own financial budget.

- This will require an updated review of our offered services and programs, and a careful review of the pricing we publish.

- More research needs to be done with how we publish and communicate our pricing to potential client customers.

# Potential Risks

- **Creative license**
- **Ill preparedness**
- **Over commitment**
- **Under commitment**
- **Stay legal and up to date**
- **Guaranteed services**

### (1) Creative License

We must always keep our focus on developing our own materials and must not ever allow ourselves to plagiarize the work of others. Credit must be given their due to whom it belongs to at all times.

A single lawsuit that requires defending will bring the entire enterprise down.

### (2) Ill Preparedness

DO NOT allow myself to commit to any initiative unless properly prepared to do so. Continue working hard to edit materials to eliminate mistakes that attack the credibility of my knowledge and performance claims. "Get ready, get set, go!"

### (3) Over Commitment

Committing to more than I can deliver is one of the very biggest risks at this point and must be avoided. No commitments will be agreed to or signed outside of the current free offering of professional advice before the basic infrastructure of materials for the services and programs offered are fully completed.

As part of this demand to be fully ready and prepared before moving forward we must make sure that the computer based systems we intend to use in presentations are also fully tested and ready for use. A test drive of sorts might be a good idea here (such as a presentation to the Kiwanis group)

- Laptop is programmed needed program drivers and with stick drives

- Projector is operational with a presentation screen

- All attachments ready and tested (clicker, speakers, connectors, etc.)

## (4) Under Commitment

At the same time we must not allow ourselves to undervalue what we've created and have to offer. When the time comes that everything is in place we must be able to pull the trigger and commit to doing what we claim we can do.

Don't allow our eye on a nonexistent or negative cash flow budget to miss opportunities that come before us (Jennifer's input will be key here).

## (5) Stay Legal and Up to Date

Stay focused on what the applicable IRS and state of Colorado rules and regulations are. If and when sales and revenues coming in make it necessary, be sure we are fully up to date with all tax application and reporting obligations (see #5 Regulations in the previous Business Strategy chapter). We can't afford the fines and penalties we could incur by failing to do so.

## (6) Guaranteed Services

While it's important that we stand behind what we do in a manner that fully supports our claim to be a "different kind of training consultant" it's just as important that we make sure the guarantees we make are credible, achievable and functional. For these reasons we should:

- Complete a full review of both the "Opt Out" and "Guaranteed Service" guarantees to make sure they apply as intended and work to our benefit without offering too much risk.

- Make any revisions needed to make them more functional, marketable, and less risky.

- Review all program agreements before signing to make sure the credibility, achievability, and functionality pieces are all in place.

By its very nature, risk is part of doing business and should never be shied away from. To not take a risk is to not harness an opportunity as the saying goes. That said, we owe it to the success of our business to understand and recognize the risks we take and do what we can to mitigate and minimize them.

# A Peek at 2016

- **Make or break year**
- **Infrastructure of services mature**
- **Client base**
- **Potential growth areas**

### (1) Make or Break Year

As we attempt to project ourselves into the future I would predict that 2016 will represent a make or break year for TRAIN2WIN where we either get fully on board with the programs and services we promise with the credible clients we identify, or simply shut the formal business side of things down to become only an information sharing enterprise.

### (2) Infrastructure of Services Mature

By 2016 all aspects of the materials and services we offer in our portfolio (we call it our infrastructure) should and must be fully mature and in place. This is not to say that we won't be on the constant lookout for additions, improvements and / or revisions to what we've created and developed.

- Amazon.com books and publications

- Relevant power point presentations where required

What will be important by 2016 is that we will by then have identified the most functional parts of the revenue generating services we want to offer so that we can properly focus our attention on marketing them to potential clients.

### (3) Client Base

According to our projected plan we should have no less than at least one full time client in our stable by the end of 2015 and the start of 2016. If that in fact does take place as projected and we have also the opportunity to use any significant part of 2015 to test and verify our methods, then the hope would be that we can begin to expand our client base more aggressively during 2016.

The mantra should be: "Don't let ourselves overachieve, but not underachieve"

**(4) Potential Growth Areas**

- Are there better ways to market the publications we create than simply listing them on Amazon.com and its distribution partners in hopes that somebody will find them?

- The entire realm of "self study" offers another potential opportunity where we design and offer complete training packages that include all of the instructional information, workbooks where applicable, and measuring devices to be used to determine the results. This in fact could ultimately redirect the TRAIN2WIN business model from the current reliance on the basic assumption that we do fully unique on site partnered analysis with the client, shared developments of customized materials, and direct TTT training, to one that offers prepackaged purchased materials. The risk here is that it gets us away from our original mission statement that states a commitment to responding to what the client needs and begins to look more like a classic consultant.

- In the same direction, You Tube offers the same sort of opportunity where tools and services can be created for posting to be watched by participants and interested parties. The key here is how the creative ownership and revenue stream would work.

- Strong consideration should be given to identifying industry trade fairs where I can network the programs and services we offer. This, of course, would require a significant investment to create a "trade booth experience" that would not only be active and dynamic, but would offer take home items to interested parties.

# Appendix A
## (TRAIN2WIN Publications)

TRAIN2WIN Manifesto

TRAIN2WIN Presentation Guide

TRAIN2WIN No Harassment Zone Publication

TRAIN2WIN Making Winning Presentations Publication

TRAIN2WIN Why Training Fails Publication

TRAIN2WIN Coach to Win Publication

All of the listed TRAIN2WIN books and publications are currently available for purchase at Amazon.com and it's distribution partners. Each of the books and publications are also available on downloadable stick drive for purchase by contacting TRAIN2WIN directly.

Where applicable (No Harassment Zone and Making Winning Presentations for example) the publication guide is supported by a matching power point that can be presented as a support tool or as a presentation of it's own.

# Appendix B
## (Forms and Reports)

TRAIN2WIN Letterhead

TRAIN2WIN Survey Analysis Package

TRAIN2WIN Agreement to Proceed

Expense & Revenue General Ledger

Individual Client Ledger

Project Planning Ledger

Record of Billable Hours

Client Claim Notice

TRAIN2WIN Billing Invoice

Monthly Income Statement

Monthly Cash Flow Report

Balance Sheet

Annual Report

# Appendix C
## (Marketing Packages)

TRAIN2WIN About Us Packet

Opt Out & Guaranteed Performance Agreements

SPEAK2WIN Packet

TRAIN2WIN Mission Statement

TRAIN2WIN Oath

Property of *TRAIN2WIN LLC* 2015.
All rights reserved.
No part of this program, or any component of such, written or verbal, may be reproduced without prior written approval from *TRAIN2WIN LLC*, except within the specified terms of any agreements signed by *TRAIN2WIN LLC*, its partners, and its clients.

www.ingramcontent.com/pod-product-compliance
Lightning Source LLC
Chambersburg PA
CBHW041619180526
45159CB00002BC/921